Someone Has To Say It

Michelle Bergquist
CEO & Co-Founder | Connected Women of Influence
Co-Founder | SUE Talks
Founding Partner | Women Lead Publishing
Co-Founder | SUE Rising
Radio and TV Host | Author | Speaker

women lead
PUBLISHING™

women lead
EXCURSIONS™

Should you speak up or not? For female leaders, there's some interesting rhetoric and debate about when to speak up and say something when you have insights to share. There's also constant debate and discussions over how to speak up and how to be heard.

What I don't see much discussion on is when to be silent and just listen. We're told, as women, we need to speak up. We need to be heard. We need to find our voice.

Yet, many times, the best method for gaining acceptance and being heard is to be silent and just listen. Really, truly listen to what's been said by others.

I never realized how much information and great insight I missed when all I focused on was when and how I needed to speak up and be heard. I was so busy trying to collect and organize my thoughts to chime in with my ideas, I missed what others were saying and I missed the opportunity to really contribute in a meaningful way.

What's so amazing about listening intently is that you capture insight and ideas differently than when you're constantly looking for when to speak up and chime in just to be heard. You're not making the greatest impact you can.

There is huge value in timing your feedback and shared insight. Taking a few notes while listening intently served me well. It gave me the opportunity to wait for a lull in conversation and then contribute in a more meaningful way with my insight, based on what was discussed and shared previously.

I found with the right timing, and waiting for the right opportunity to speak, my ideas were accepted much more frequently and the contribution and discussion made a greater impact.

As a leader, until I learned to be silent and just listen, I missed so much great information and never realized how much I missed in content and ideas!

So the next time you're in a situation where you're looking to speak up, just stop and listen. Truly listen in with both ears to what the other person, or group, is sharing.

I promise, you'll be amazed with the results!

One incredible evening!

Join us to hear bold, passionate and inspiring talks by successful, unstoppable and empowering leaders.

Hear their experiences, journeys, passions, opinions, and their pursuits.

October 12, 2021
"Find Your Fierce" | San Diego

December 7, 2021
"The Leader Within" | Orange County

May 12, 2022
"I Got This!" | Los Angeles

July 20, 2022
"That Little Extra" | Inland Empire

September 29, 2022
"Just Because" | San Diego

December 6, 2022
"Feel the Fear" | Orange County

Interested in bringing SUE Talks to your community? Call 800.591.1673

www.suetalks.com Talks that inspire change.™

brought to you by: connected women OF INFLUENCE

women lead ™

A Publication of: Women Lead Publishing

Brought to you by:

Connected Women of Influence (CWI)

We are a professional association of women who lead people, projects, teams and companies.

Our Passion & Mission

To advance and elevate female leaders in business, industry and enterprise.

lead...
achieve...
succeed...

together

www.connectedwomenofinfluence.com

SUE TALKS™ | partners

Michelle Bergquist
Co-Founder and
Chief Empire Builder

Michelle Bergquist is a nationally recognized author, award-winning entrepreneur, lively moderator and engaging, professional speaker. Michelle is a passionate advocate to advance women in business, and committed to designing platforms, programs, connections and collaborative opportunities that result in more women leading people, projects, teams, and companies. With a passion to 'give back' in business, Michelle's philanthropic efforts have resulted in over $300,000 in contributions for local nonprofit organizations that support women and young girls.
Something I've always wanted to try:
Flying as a guest with the Blue Angels!

Deanna Potter, M.A.
Co-Founder and
Chief Inspiration Officer

Deanna Potter is the Strategic Communications Manager for The Centre for Organization Effectiveness. Deanna has over 25 years' experience in individual coaching and group training courses designed to improve organizational results. She is a speaker, trainer, coach, and author who has consulting experience in both the private and public sectors. She understands the demands and importance of balancing an organization's key performance objectives against the welfare of the individuals within the organization.
Favorite guilty pleasure:
A spray tan and a good martini!

Linda Amaro
Chief Vision Officer

Linda Amaro drives the innovation that continually propels Klarinet to meet peak performance goals. Over her career, she has built data centers from the ground up and spearheaded building the infrastructure for virtual offices and teams. She's also got some serious people skills - meet her and you'll quickly realize how she turns the stereotype of quiet, withdrawn IT professionals on its head. The queen of achieving career fulfillment and work-life balance, when Linda shuts the corporate door, she shifts to be an engaged grandmother and non-profit board member.
Something most people don't know about me:
I am a furniture designer with global clients!

Sashi Whitman
Chief Legacy Officer

Sashi Whitman is an educator and teaches market research at UCSD Extension for international students, and business and marketing courses at San Diego Miramar College. Her background is in marketing, specifically market research and product management. She has worked overseas in Saudi Arabia and the United Arab Emirates, where she sold American luxury goods to the Middle East market. Sashi is passionate about empowering young girls and women to build confidence, find their voice and create influence that breaks barriers globally.
Favorite business book: Seth Godin's *Tribes!*

Thank You to our SUE Talks Coaches!

1. Jen Shen	5. Ana Nieto	9. Michelle Beauchamp	13. Christine Cunliffe
2. Charlesetta Medina	6, Adrienne Grace	10. Analia Mendez	14. Dianne Callahan
3. Lizzie Wittig	7. Zhe Scott	11. Knight Campbell	15. Kay Trotman
4. Michele Farrell	8. Mary Van Dorn	12. LaVonne Shields	16. Lenka Holman

Mary Barnett
www.anotherbrilliantidea.com

Mary Barnett, known as "MobileMary" in the industry, is a Text Marketing Expert and a Mobile/Social Conversationalist and loves sharing her passion, innovative strategies and expertise on LIVE weekly video training on her Facebook page (TheMobileMary) #TextingTuesdays at 3 pm. Mary is also a Keynote Speaker on stages in-person and virtual for companies, industry associations, and business groups. She loves being a guest on podcasts as she offers action-packed value for listeners, and they always smile as they hear her "contagious enthusiasm" during broadcasts!

Mary helps her clients be as awesome online as they have been offline for years!

"MobileMary" is the immediate past-President of the American Marketing Association and also the owner of a certified woman-owned small business called Another Brilliant Idea, Inc., which has been a boutique marketing firm since 1988, with expertise in various online and offline marketing channels that have created brilliant results for their online, restaurant, retail, corporate, city and military clientele.

Fun Facts About Mary

I am the original "Burger Queen"....
When I was in 2nd grade, my sister worked for Burger King and they had a float in the Anaheim Halloween Parade (a big event in the old days) so she made me a giant dress from dyed sheets and lots of puffy slips, and I sat at the top of the float to wave at the crowds, and they chanted "Burger Queen, Burger Queen, Yay!" So yes, I have that going for me!

Barbara Berg

www.barbaraberg.com

Truly committed to bringing dignity, kindness, and concern to people, Barbara A. Berg has found social work to be the perfect profession. Today, Ms. Berg continues to make strides as a speaker, award-winning author, and licensed clinical social worker.

In her private practice, Ms. Berg specializes in helping her clients live their lives more authentically and have "successful midlife crises." She also provides marriage counseling, relationship counseling, and help for those in transition in their careers and life.

As a testament to her hard work and dedication, Ms. Berg has received numerous accolades over the years. Most notably, she was honored with the President's Lifetime Achievement Award from President Obama for her lifelong commitment to building a stronger nation through volunteer services in 2015.

Ms. Berg loves having the privilege of working with people as they grow and achieve their goals; seeing firsthand how resilient and compassionate people can be, even in turbulent times, has really inspired her. Looking to the future, she hopes to continue her work and connect with larger audiences around the world.

Fun Facts About Barbara

The time I felt totally unstoppable, was the day I had an amazingly wonderful time as a guest for my first book, "What to Do When Life is Driving You Crazy!" on the Howard Stern Show in the morning, and got a call from Oprah's producers on the same afternoon. I never did get Oprah, but on that very day I truly felt unstoppable!

Deena C. Brown

www.leadhershiftmovement.com

Dr. Deena C.Brown is a peak performance strategist, author, and speaker helping entrepreneurs, and enterprises maximize their effectiveness by navigating mindset, marketing, and monetization perils from ideation to implementation.

Dr. Brown has been working in Organizational Development, Executive Coaching, Organizational Change & Transformation, and Leadership Development for over 20 years. As a certified human behavioral analysis consultant, she teaches leaders to engage, motivate and develop their people successfully.

Dr. Brown leads people to discover, maximize and lead with their strengths. Dr. Brown knows first-hand how strengths and leadership are keys to business effectiveness and growth. Her skills were honed over two decades as an educator and school administrator with the Department of Defense.

Dr. Brown's vision and vast diversity, equity, inclusion, and belonging strategy for enhancing organizational culture help enterprises harness human capital's power to embrace diversity and inclusion as an integral aspect of innovation and advancement.

Fun Facts About Deena

The best business advice I have received has been from John Hope Bryant: "There are three types of people in this world: Thriver, Survivor, and Winner. It's up to you to decide which one you're going to be."

My favorite business book is Think and Grow Rich. The essence of building a solid business and thriving is having the right mindset.

Sharleen Lawrence

www.empirewellnesscenter.com

Sharleen earned her Master's degree in Traditional Oriental Medicine in 2014. Her path to helping people achieve wellness began in 2005 while practicing the Japanese art of Seifukujutsu massage. During her massage training, she learned about Asian Medicine and Acupuncture, and it resonated so powerfully, she knew she had found her calling. Sharleen attended the prestigious Emperor's College in Santa Monica, CA where she graduated magna cum laude. Sharleen has a broad range of clinical experience, which includes treating addiction, supporting mental health, digestive disorders, thyroid health, autoimmune conditions, and fertility.

After being inspired by watching the documentary Heal, she completed a 500-hour training program in hypnotherapy. She finds that combining acupuncture with hypnotherapy in her HypnoPuncture treatments allows the patient to achieve healing on all three levels of mind, body, and soul. The effectiveness of her HypnoPuncture treatments motivated her to develop the HypnoPuncture Method and in early 2021, Sharleen started teaching her method to other licensed acupuncturists around the world.

Fun Facts About Sharleen

I've been a long-distance runner since 2008 and I enjoy pushing the limits of my body with yoga and pilates. One thing I've always wanted to do is run a marathon at the Great Wall of China. It would be the biggest physical challenge I've ever done, for sure.

Joseph Molina

www.theveteranschamber.org

Jospeh Molina is an Army veteran currently serving as Executive Director/CEO for the Veterans Chamber of Commerce.

Mr. Molina has over 12 years' experience as a business and leadership advisor with extensive experience in business concepts, start-up process, strategies, supervisory concepts and new leadership strategies. He is Co-Founder of Alliance Funding Group, a micro-enterprise that supports micro businesses who need initial funding to start their business.

Mr. Molina founded MetroCollegeOnline in 2005, a private training platform that provides entrepreneurship and employee leadership training to organizations.

Since 1998, Mr. Molina has been a faculty member for Park University as well teaching at universities and community colleges, including courses on management and veterans in agriculture at Cal Poly Pomona and entrepreneurship at MiraCosta College.

Fun Facts About Jospeh

Three tips/strategies I share with leaders to help them make their mark and advance in business:

1. **Know what you want and keep moving forward towards it (you are 90% there)**

2. **Only work with positive people (the others are toxic)**

3. **Practice visualization to see your vision clearly**

Joan Stanford

jazzypen.com

Joan Stanford transforms the way business owners and entrepreneurs think about using words to market their businesses. As the founder of Jazzy Pen Communications, a marketing communications firm specializing in content marketing, she works with busy entrepreneurs to build their brands and craft content that attracts their ideal customers.

With a journalism background and an inquisitive mind, Joan's a master at getting to the heart of a company's message and weaving that message into compelling copy that gets results. The award-winning business owner has more than 20 years of professional writing, editing and marketing experience in a diverse array of industries including manufacturing, software technology, and market research, to name a few.

A highly sought-after speaker, Joan has spoken for several business groups and conferences such as the SBA in Los Angeles, Inland Empire Women's Business Center, and the National Latina Women's Business Association. Her dynamic presentations and workshops are full of energy and participants walk away with a new zeal for the written word and for marketing.

Fun Facts About Joan

One of my favorite business books is The 10X Rule by Grant Cardone. I listened to it on audible and absolutely loved Grant's energy and straightforward nature. Plus the information was good, actionable advice.

The best piece of business advice I ever received is "Run your business. Don't let it run you."

Sharron Stroud

www.innerfaithworldwide.com

Fun Facts About Sharron

My first job was modeling at age 16 with the Rita La Roy Modelling School and Agency in Encino, CA.

The best advice I've ever received: "Anybody who succeeds is helping people. The secret to success is find a need and fill it; find a hurt and heal it; find a problem and solve it."
- The Rev. Dr. Robert Schuller

Dr. Sharron Stroud is a woman dedicated to serving the planet. The slogan "Think Globally and Act Locally" would describe what she has been about for the past 46 years. She is an author, professional speaker, and a spiritual leader. She has served the New Thought movement for 46 years as a spiritual leader.

Dr. Stroud serves as the Spiritual Leader of Innerfaith Spiritual Center Worldwide in Palm Springs, CA. since 2001. She also serves as the Dean of the Institute of Successful Living.

Dr. Stroud is the President Elect of The International Foundation for World Peace and Research, in which she travels all over the world lecturing at Universities and Institutions of Learning. Most recently at the Cultural Arts Festival in India in January, The International Congress on Art, Science, Communication and Technology in Edinburgh, Scotland, Madonna University in Nigeria, Africa, the University of Istanbul Medical Center in Turkey, The University of Zagreb in Croatia, The University of African and Oriental Studies in London, England, Essen, Germany, Queen's College in Cambridge England and Oslo, Norway where she served on the Nobel Peace Prize Nominating Commission.

Liane Barkhordar

SUE Riser

Liane Barkhordar is a current senior at University City High School. She will be graduating this June with a 4.58 GPA. At University City High School, Liane plays on the varsity lacrosse team and is president of the homeless outreach club.

In her free time she enjoys making earrings, watching the sunset, and spending time with her family and friends. Liane will be continuing her education at UCSD next year where she will be studying political science on a pre-law track. She also aspires to do a minor in business.

What do you think more young girls need to know about their future?

If you are thinking about a career in business, start exploring your hobbies and grow one or more into a small business. I did this by expanding on my hobby of making earrings and developed this into a business. This hands-on experience really taught me about the business world. I learned the best way to market my earrings, manage my finances and sales, and even how to sustainably package my products. This same concept can be applied to a range of hobbies from baking, doing nails or even teaching a sport. Whatever you choose to do, I say the best tip is to get hands on, and take things step by step!

Fun Facts About Liane

I have always wanted to try paragliding at the gliderport in San Diego. I have always wonderedwhat it's like to fly like a bird, and paragliding is the best way to experience this unique point of view. It has always seemed very peaceful to me and it seems very cool to be able to see all of San Diego under my feet.

SUE Riser

Alison Kokorowski

Fun Facts About Alison

My favorite guilty pleasure is eating a pint of strawberry ice cream and watching a movie.

I have always wanted to go skydiving just to feel the rush of falling from super high and seeing the earth from above.

Most people don't know that I have been stung by stingray

Alison Kokorowski is a sophomore at Mira Costa High School who enjoys playing water polo and singing with her friends. She also loves to spend time at the beach and on a rainy day you can catch her curled up with a good book. Her first job was pre-COVID over the summer when she worked as an assistant camp counselor at her aerial arts studio. There she supervised and taught younger kids how to do things on the silks and trapeze. Some of Alison's best leadership qualities include her confidence, self awareness, empathy, communication, responsibility, and honesty. Alison is excited to be a SUE Rising talker because she is so happy for the opportunity to step outside her comfort zone and practice her public speaking skills at a higher level.

What is one trait or behavior that you feel has helped you succeed the most?
One trait that constantly helps me succeed in school is being positive. Especially because of COVID, school has been a lot more stressful but it has been really beneficial to maintain a positive attitude as I move through my day.

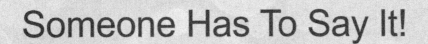

Someone Has To Say It!

"The only way to be heard is to actually speak up."

"Speak up. Believe in yourself. Take risks."

"Speak your mind even though your voice shakes."
~ Eleanor Roosevelt

Bluechild Entertainment is an all-encompassing entertainment entity. Be it film, television, music or photography production, our products and programming are always high quality and marketable.

Since we are a boutique production company, we are able to be hands-on in facilitating programming that is unique and original.

We can handle your production for independent commercials, music videos, films, web series, and television. We can even help you develop and shoot footage for your acting reel. Every member of our team works professionally in the film and television industry. We will help you polish your script, put together your crew, edit and score your video providing you with a polished, professional project.

Call us
818 350-3866

bluechildentertainment.
com

If you are a singer, poet or just want beautiful family photos, our photography department can provide you with photographs to meet all your needs. If you are an actor who needs headshots, we can coach you through your headshot session to get the exact look you need to book your next job. Do you want to take sexy photos for your significant other? We can assist you with that too.

Sky is the limit when it comes to giving you quality service at a reasonable price.

connected women
OF INFLUENCE®

Connected Women of Influence (CWI) is a national association of women leading people, projects, teams or companies who connect, collaborate and cultivate a vast network of high-level affiliations, resources and professional relationships.

Our Mission:
To build a strong, professional community that fosters growth, support and collaboration through the development of high-performing professional relationships, alliances and partnerships among female owners, executives and professionals.

Why We Exist:
We believe that professional women converging together with the sole purpose of supporting one another professionally leads to better advocacy on behalf of each other.

Our philosophy is that professional support, advocacy, partnerships and alliances lead to better business opportunities, and better business opportunities lead to finding increased value, which results in phenomenal growth and business success!

Our Vision:
To see more women lead the way in business!

The #1 thing to kickstart your speaking today

The #1 thing to kickstart (or reboot) your speaking to attract many more ideal clients is… to book yourself to speak!

Seriously.

Even if you don't have a signature talk yet (or it's not where you want it to be).

Even if you're not completely clear on your offer.

Even if you're still deciding on your niche.

Even if you feel shaky about speaking, or you don't feel "ready."

Because when you book yourself to speak–on a podcast, an interview series or a Zoom networking group–you have a date, a deadline to work towards.

Having a date to work towards gets you out of the "When I get my talk really polished and put together, then I'll put myself out there more and book myself to speak."

Noooooooooo.

Book a date, and then you'll have a very compelling reason to create or polish your talk (and get support for putting it all together).

It doesn't have to be THE big speaking opportunity of the century. We're not talking Oprah, the TED (or SUE!) stage, or a big networking group, unless you're ready and wanting that.

It could be something small: a podcast interview with a friend or colleague or gathering 10 of your biggest fans and supporters in a Zoom room to share your wisdom and a simple call to action.

That's exactly how I started nine years ago: 10 people in my chiropractor's waiting room. And I got clients, even though I wasn't a very polished or confident speaker in those days.

Saying "yes" to speaking and booking yourself to speak is saying a big YES to you and your desire to be seen, to be heard and to receive an abundance of clients, money and opportunities in your business.

Are you in?

Rebecca Massoud is a contributing writer for Women Lead Publications, where she covers all things speaking, visibility and client attraction for women entrepreneurs. Rebecca inspires thousands to share their brilliance on stage as a speaker coach. Her clients courageously step into the spotlight with a soulful signature talk, attract their ideal clients with ease, and double (or triple!) their revenue, as they unapologetically say "yes" to being seen, heard and highly visible. www.rebeccamassoud.com

Selfishness is your most important (and most ignored) superpower

I have a book in my library that I bought for the cover alone. I don't even need to read this one. Everything I need to know about it is right there in five bright red words on the front of the book.

NO is a Complete Sentence by Megan LeBoutillier. What more needs to be said?

The title is a great reminder that we all have the right to declare boundaries of what we are willing to do, and accept, at the actions/requests of others. And, we can declare those boundaries in just two letters: N-O. Period.

I forget this sometimes. That's why I bought the book and have it facing out on my shelf. Some days, I need that powerful reminder that I can be selfish and say "No."

The problem with saying "No" is that other people tend not to appreciate it when we say it.

They want our help, or think they need something from us, and when we refuse, they get upset…maybe they even accuse us of being uncaring and (gasp)

selfish. Which of course can make us then feel bad, so we cave in and say "OK" (which is a wimpy yes), and then we feel even worse. In the short-term, they get what they want and we feel bad in both the short- and long-terms.

Ugh.

So how can you give yourself permission to be selfish and say "NO?'

1. Take a breath, slow down, and listen to your gut instinct. What does your intuition tell you to do?

2. If your intuition is telling you to say "No," then know that it's OK to say it. It is your personal right.

3. Take the action of saying it. Practice it. I invite you to say it with me now: NO. (Didn't that feel good?)

4. If the other person says you are selfish, remember your gut said "No" and stand in the power of your declaration.

Stop weakening yourself by saying "Yes" all the time. Give yourself permission to be selfish and say "NO." I promise, you'll feel like a superhero.

Daniel Olexa is a contributing writer for Women Lead Publications, where he coaches Dead People. His gift is to bring them back to life by breathing new air into their life story, as they exhale what they no longer need. He is a 3-time Amazon #1 Bestselling author, life coach trainer, keynote speaker, award-winning hypnotherapist, holistic entrepreneur, and Transcendent Living coach serving international clients from his home base in the Los Angeles area. www.danielolexa.com

Have you thought about the future?

As a female business owner, how much planning goes into taking a week vacation? Leaving your business, even for a short period of time, takes planning. Unfortunately, many business owners plan for their vacations, but not for the future of their business.

Business succession involves creating a plan for who will take over your business in the event of your retirement, death or disability. A successor could be a person inside the company. Maybe a key manager, employee or it could be a family member. The successor may be an outside person or entity. Naming a successor reduces the possibility of a dispute in the

future. In addition to selecting who to transfer ownership to, business owners need to train the new owner on how to run the business.

Business succession is more than simply choosing the successor. It is about ensuring that you are ready to exit your business should an opportunity present itself. With that in mind it is essential to a smooth transition to ensure that financial documents are consolidated. This includes company valuation data, inventory, tax returns and up-to-date financial records. Potential buyers and lenders will want to see how the business has performed historically before proceeding with a deal.

The business should have a buy-sell agreement in place. These agreements address what will occur in the business should the owner pass away, become ill, or retire. This agreement provides a guideline to determine the value of the company, the value of each owners' share and rules on who can or cannot be a buyer. This agreement also reduces the risk of conflicts between family members or partners who may put their interests ahead of the company's.

Proper succession planning calls for careful consideration and preparation. While it may be difficult to entertain the thought of exiting the business, unexpected circumstances can force an early exit. Whether someone is nearing retirement age or just beginning, business owners should take time now to build a succession plan that protects their business' longevity and secures their financial future.

Kariann Voorhees is a contributing writer for Women Lead Publications, where she covers all topics on estate planning and business succession planning. Kariann Voorhees has been an estate planning attorney for over 8 years and is a Certified Exit Planner (CEPA). She is the managing partner of Voorhees & Ratzlaff Law Group, LLP Her firm provides comprehensive, highly personalized estate planning counsel and business succession planning.www.vrlawgroup.com

Someone Has To Say It!

"A lot of people are afraid to say what they want. That's why they don't get what they want."

"You cannot be afraid to speak up and speak out for what you believe. You have to have courage, raw courage."
~ John Lewis

We all want to be SUE

We do. We all want to be SUE. Who is SUE, you ask? SUE is a successful, unstoppable, empowering woman changing the face of business. Don't you think we all want to be that?

I want to be SUE. I want to be more successful. Every day I strive to better my best, get back up when I fall, strive for greatness and never settle for anything short of excellence. Not perfection, but excellence.

I definitely want to be unstoppable, especially when dealing with obstacles or adversity. I want to never stop, never give up and keep doing the very best I can every day and in every way.

I also want to be empowered, to feel like I have the power and influence to create change and make a difference. I want to create and take charge of my future as a professional woman.

In addition to feeling empowered, I believe it's also critical to empower other women to be stronger, bolder and more confident, empowering them to believe in taking charge of their future!

When you're SUE, you're changing the face of business. **When you're more successful, more unstoppable and more empowered, the face of business changes.** With more SUE, there will be more females in power positions in business and industry, more women leaders and more women serving on boards and holding senior management positions.

Here's to SUE! Let's all be SUE!

__Michelle Bergquist__ is the Co-Founder and CEO of Connected Women of Influence, as well as Chief Publisher for Women Lead Publications. Michelle is a passionate advocate for advancing women in business and believes more women can and should lead the way in business, industry and enterprise. Connected Women of Influence (CWI) is a national, invitation only association where women owners, executives and professionals connect, collaborate and cultivate a vast network of high-level affiliations, resources and professional relationships. www.connectedwomenofinfluence.com

Set and get your goals

We are now in the second half of the year, so my purpose with these tips is to equip you with some tools to not only set your goals, but to achieve them!

Start with your why.

Do your goals inspire you, or do they feel like heavy weights and excess responsibility? How do your goals align with your passion? (In the last few months there's been increased discussion about people evaluating their current positions and whether they're fulfilling their passion and purpose).

When you wake up in the morning how exhilarated are you to get the day started to get closer to your goals? Know your why, start with why.

Tools that may help you clarify your why:

1) Imagine – yes, be willing to imagine. This will require you to STOP- dream and let your imagination run away with you. When I knew I wanted to launch my company and was at my corporate job, I imagined what it would feel like, sound like and look like. Allow yourself to visualize and imagine.

2) Inventory what's holding you back – In other words, what's the pebble in your shoe? When you are running or walking and you feel that pebble in your shoe, the only way to keep your pace is to stop, untie your shoe and remove it, shake the pebble out, and put the shoe back on and lace up so you can regain your momentum. Discover what's holding you back so you can get back in stride.

3) Inventory who you are hanging out with – are you associating with others who have the same or higher motives as you do that inspire you and propel you?

4) Assess who you intend to become –The book, Atomic Habits by James Clear and 15 Laws of Invaluable Growth by John Maxwell home in on this point.

I wish you all the success you can handle as you establish your goals. Stay growth conscious. Go get what is waiting for you.

 Michelle Beauchamp is a contributing writer for Women Lead Publications, where she is the CEO of The Champ Group, a certified coach, speaker and trainer on the John Maxwell team. Michelle's 25 years in Corporate America as a Sales Leader in Telecommunications, combined with her 10 + years as an entrepreneur, has equipped her to help others explore their strengths, improve areas of weakness and through a journey of inner discovery, create diverse and inclusive cultures that enrich relationships and increase productivity. www.beasaleschamp.net

Join Us on Our Next Excursion!

Build Amazing Professional Relationships!

Bond With Other Professional Women!

Socialize While Making New Connections!

Fun! Fun! FUN!

www.womenleadexcursions.com

Upcoming dates:

Thursday, August 12
Long Beach Harbor Cruise | Wine Down

Thursday, November 11
Temecula Valley Wine Tasting | Dinner
Balloon Ride

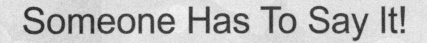

Someone Has To Say It!

*"Have you ever wondered which hurts the most:
saying something and wishing you had not,
or saying nothing and wishing you had?"*

*"Women speaking up for themselves,
and for those around them is the strongest force
we have to change the world."*
~ Melinda Gates

Recovering from our childhood

What if we are all in the process of recovering from our childhood? If so, it shouldn't take us years and thousands of dollars to process it. There is no need to spend time wallowing in it. We can be honest with ourselves about our childhood and what it is: the past.

Generally speaking, as kids, we didn't learn how to love our selves. Our parents didn't either because they weren't shown. We came into this world as babies so pure! Then we begin intuitively picking up silent messages along the way. We take our first hurt and drag it with us through our life.

Here's the deal: it wasn't our fault. We are not bad. We were innocent children dealing with all of the dynamics around us the best we could.

When I was a little girl, I remember my mom being very emotional. I don't recall how that showed up in my life, but I remember making a choice not to be "weak" like her.

When my dad suddenly died of a heart attack at 49, I was 21 years old and I would not let myself feel the depths of any pain or grief. I was so scared…if I

let myself feel the pain, I would end up in a mental hospital. I would never stop crying and feeling sad, I'd go crazy, and I would be institutionalized forever. I just knew it.

Fast forward ten years later…I would still get a lump in my throat, and I knew it was time to face my dad's death. Scary stuff! I reached out to a hypnotherapist and there I began healing my grief.

I learned there are different phases we go through to heal. We can process our grief and come out on the other end without being institutionalized.

What is unresolved in your life now that is a direct result of silent messages from your childhood?

Our past experiences color the way we respond to situations today. Are you ready to give yourself a chance, forgive and be the glorious human being you were born to be

Jodie Moncrief is a contributing writer for Women Lead Publications. With her well-rounded background and passion for growth in herself and others, Jodie facilitates online workshops on "Self-Worth through Core Empowerment," "10 Ways to Grow Your Business," "Living a Balanced Life," "10 Ways to Health & Wellness," and "Building Confident Children," among others. Jodie was born in San Diego and currently resides in Mission Viejo, California with her husband of 35 years. She is director for the Orange County Global Society of Female Entrepreneurs.

SUE
TALKS

The passion behind SUE Talks is to showcase successful, unstoppable and empowering women who are changing the face of business. In one evening, a group of hand-selected, well-rehearsed women each share a SUE Talk that is passionate, bold and brief with their stories and viewpoints, as well as their journey, of business and success.

"It's women's time," says Michelle. "It's time for the business community to hear the thoughts and ideas women have on advancement and how to be successful in business."

Why SUE? Deanna suggested the name SUE that first day. But Michelle had to be sure. "We spent days and hours looking up every female name we could find," she said. "We even talked about whether it should be 'SUE Talks' or 'SUE Speaks.' " In the end, SUE translated into "Successful," "Unstoppable" and "Empowered."

Talks that inspire change

"Why don't we do our own version of talks by women focusing on women's advancement in business?"

— Deanna Potter
SUE Talks Co-Founder

The next step was branding. "Real" and "authentic" are the operative words. "We want this to be by real women and for real women. Real women doing real things in real situations in business," Michelle offers.

Adds Deanna, "It's about sharing the struggles and obstacles and adversity. It's not about telling the world, 'here's my 5 tips on how you should be successful.'"

"SUE Talks," says Michelle, "are about passion and purpose, ambition and lessons learned. It should be a conversation, as though you're having a one-on-one with a colleague or a friend. It's not about telling. It's about sharing a person's story, hardship, adversity or success, and what they learned from the experience that benefits you, the listener."

"SUE Talks give women the confidence to be OK being real," adds Deanna, "so they don't have to pretend that everything is perfect and they have to do it perfectly all the time. Everyone out there has some sort of trial, tragedy or obstacle – and they come out the other side the better for it, with lessons from the experience."

They banned visual aids such as PowerPoint ("death by bullet point," Michelle calls it) as well as note cards. "It's a performance. It's rehearsed, polished and presented with passion," Michelle says. For SUE Talkers, it's a unique experience. SUE Talks are both a professional growth experience and an opportunity to make deep connections with fellow SUE Talkers also working through the process.

"They are a club of their own," says Michelle. Adds Deanna, "They have put in months of time, emotion and effort just for that 12 minutes. And whether they've been on stage before or had the experience of presenting, most of them have never given this kind of talk before. They haven't stood up and said, 'I lived through a divorce. I went through this in business.

Here's what I learned from this and how you can apply this to business.' It's bold and different and empowering!"

The lead-up to a SUE Talk is rigorous. SUE Talkers pen their speech, practice it – then participate in a pair of mandatory run-throughs. It's not meant to be perfect at the dry run, where the talkers get advice on everything from body language to adding details or improving the imagery to make more of an impact.

"We want people to be inspired and empowered," says Deanna. Michelle adds,

"We want women to be brave enough to say, 'I want to stand up on that stage and give the most incredible and passionate talk of my professional life.' "

What do you think - really?

I have been in hot pursuit of the potential riches that lie in wait for those who can truly get a handle on their thoughts. Be aware: this is no easy task! An untrained mind is like an untrained dog: chaotic, rude, driven by impulse, and inclined to be harmful to self and others. And most of the time we're not even aware that this is happening.

As part of my renewed focus on managing my thoughts, I have been going through some lessons and meditations in a program created by Dr. Joe Dispenza, renowned chiropractor, neuroscientist, lecturer, and best-selling author. In a nutshell, he teaches people how to program their brains (through conscious thought, emotion, and meditation) for the outcomes they desire in their lives. One of the most important steps in this process is the practice of becoming acutely aware of one's own thoughts.

Take a moment to consider this: have you ever really thought about your thoughts? Have you ever really paid attention, moment by moment, to all the stuff that flits through your brain?

When I did, I was stunned to discover how much of it is petty and negative. I could hear this voice chattering in an irritated tone and basically bitching non-stop about whatever circumstances I was facing in the moment. You know, things like: someone left their laundry in the dryer; the counter didn't get wiped down; oh my God, I have to think up a dinner plan again; there's no time for anything; I'm so sick of being the only one who loads the dishwasher; why is that idiot driving so fast? And on and on. Also, and aside from being generally annoyed with everything in life, I discovered that a ton of my thoughts are driven by a certain emotion: fear. Apparently, I'm afraid of everything!

The most illuminating part of this practice, though, has got to be what I discovered I think about myself:

· I am tired
· I am stupid
· I am timid
· I am afraid
· I am unworthy
· I am traumatized
· I am ridiculous
· I am unable

No, I don't think these things about myself all the time, but I was certainly able to identify some thought/emotion feedback loops, where either a thought feeds into an emotion (or vice versa), which then reinforces itself in a constant loop. I am learning to break those loops by bringing awareness to the problem, and then flipping those thoughts into what I desire: I am energized, confident, capable, accomplished, generous, courageous, authentic, and so on.

It's not enough to just realize that we really don't want to think the thoughts we've been thinking; we have to decide what we do want to think, instead.

It's a little disorienting, by the way. To pull your brain and your heart out of those old, habitual grooves can definitely cause some dissonance. Don't be deterred! Keep at it. The rewards are well worth the effort, and I can absolutely attest to the fact that I am less afraid of everything than I have been in a very long time; more productive; happier; and, honestly, more myself. Which, it turns out, is someone I don't know very well because of all the things my brain has said about me, that I don't actually need to believe.

Change your thoughts; change your life.
It really is true.

Starlene Justice is a contributing writer for Women Lead Publications. She is a writer and professor of geography at Norco College in southern California. She holds a BA in Geography and MA in Social Sciences from Cal State San Bernardino, as well an MFA in Creative Writing from National University. Her fiction and non-fiction work has appeared in various journals and magazines, and has won prizes in both local and international writing competitions. Her books, The Evangelist" and "The Astonishing Light of Your Own Being: Powerful Practices to Shape Your Future and Showcase Your Brilliance" are available on Amazon. www.starlenejustice.com

Stupid girl

I recently conducted a career workshop for leaders on how to prepare for a job interview. Twelve women and four men were in attendance. I asked, "Who wants to be the first to volunteer for a mock interview?" Four men waved their hands in the air. I was stunned that not a single woman volunteered.

After the men completed their interviews, I tried to encourage a few women to give it a try, stressing that participation would be a valuable experience. No luck. Finally, I walked over to one woman and whispered, Come on, you can do this. What's the problem?

"Everyone will think I'm stupid because I don't know how to answer these questions," she whispered. I tried to persuade her to get some courage. I'll help you. With that reassurance, she finally volunteered. Everyone clapped as she walked to the front of the room. Her interview was excellent.

Out of curiosity, I asked the men in the group why they had volunteered for the mock interview. They responded they had nothing to lose and added they were used to taking chances and didn't want to waste an opportunity to practice.

No one likes to look stupid. Many women share they are reluctant to

take a chance on something for fear of looking stupid. This problem is difficult to address since the fear of looking stupid is deeply rooted in one's psychological arena.

If you suffer from the fear of looking stupid, it's important to realize that everyone feels stupid at some point in their life.
Anticipating or expecting too much, too soon, in any endeavor can lead to failure, so it helps to be realistic with what you take on. But believing that you will fail almost guarantees failure.

Studies of successful women reveal they accept failure as inevitable and are not afraid to take a chance. Next time you feel 'stupid,' think about all the women you know who succeed at almost everything without fear. Be like them and resist the fear of feeling stupid.

Marilou Ryder is a contributing writer for Women Lead Publications, where she is a university professor, and best-selling author. She is a passionate proponent of women and girl's empowerment through evidence-based techniques. Through her writing, speaking, and research, she galvanizes others to summon their best selves to approach life's challenges by accessing their personal power. Her innovative work includes the publication of three INSTAGRAPHICS, engaging books infused with Inspirations, Hints, Tips & Truths. SHOW YOUR WORTH, GIRL is her latest Instagraphic for teen girls- available on Amazon. www.drmarilouryder.com

Someone Has To Say It!

"Don't be afraid to speak up.
Some people may not appreciate your opinion.
Others may criticize you for it. But the ones who
really matter in your life will respect you for it."

"There's a moment when you have to choose
whether to be silent or to stand up."
~ Malala Yousafzai

INVERSE PRO AUDIO

What We Do!

As a top Audio Visual Equipment Rental Service, we stock our shop with only the best rentals on the market. We aim to provide excellent customer service to all those looking for quality rentals, as well as low prices to keep them coming back time and time again.

See our amazing selection online before you come into the Audio Visual Equipment Rental Service to get an idea of what we have in stock.

Can't find what you're looking for? Get in touch with us.

Pro Audio Gear

- Microphones
- PA Systems
- Keyboards
- Synthesizers
- Drums
- Guitar Amps
- Bass Amps
- Control Board

LED Lighting

- Uplighting
- Follow Spotlight
- Moving Head Lights
- Laser & FX Lighting
- Control Board

Top reasons to invest in the cloud

Small to medium-sized businesses (SMBs) lag behind their enterprise counterparts when it comes to cloud adoption. And while cloud-based productivity apps like Office 365 have steadily grown among these smaller companies, legacy software continues to be used. Below are some of the most crucial and game-changing benefits SMBs have reported after investing in cloud solutions.

Companies that move to the cloud make more money.
And not by a small percentage, either. SMBs that invest in the cloud report up to 25% growth in revenue. Lower up-front capital costs, like the high cost of hardware and software licenses. Plus, resources are saved on software upgrades, energy costs, and underutilized computing resources.

Unparalleled business flexibility.
Cloud software allows small businesses to always remain on regardless of location. The ability to be productive on any device provides the flexibility required to adapt quickly to changing information and business needs. This means more agile operations and happier customers.

Cost-effective scalability.
SMBs need increased flexibility to grow and scale without hassle. With the cloud, as an SMB adds users, generates more transactions or adds more data, services dynamically scale to manage workload.

Improved collaboration.
Cloud-based workspaces offer more effective cooperation. Cloud computing allows teams to be productive, regardless of their location. This enables businesses to provide flexible working arrangements that create healthier work/life balance and happier employees without sacrificing productivity.

Superior security and data protection. Small businesses are the most common victims of security breaches. Businesses reported security benefits they could not achieve with their previous on-premises resources. Laptops get lost or stolen all the time. In addition to the replacement costs, the loss of critical or sensitive data is even higher. However, data is available and protected when storing and backing up data in the cloud, regardless of what happens to personal devices.

SMBs now have cloud software available to operate all business operations from a single, connected solution infused with AI and advanced analytics.

Moving to the cloud provides SMBs with access to enterprise-class technologies which allows for improved customer satisfaction, faster innovation and increased revenue.

Ready for the cloud yet?

Francine Otterson is a contributing writer for Women Lead Publications, where she is an enterprise and SMB IT veteran with over twenty-five years of experience, and was awarded Microsoft MVP for expertise in Microsoft Office. She is the owner of Service Desk West, Inc, an IT Service Provider focusing on the SMB sector, offering comprehensive business technology solutions and delivering Microsoft 365 Cloud expertise to the community via interactive consultation services. www.servicedeskwest.com

Connected.
Women.
Influence.

A few years ago, Meryl Streep accepted the Cecil B. DeMille Award for outstanding contributions to the world of entertainment at the Golden Globes. In her speech, she addressed three important aspects of the current political climate: Hollywood, foreigners and the press.

I can't help but think of this group we are all a part of: Connected Women of Influence. So – as Meryl did – allow me to break down my interpretation of Connected, Women and Influence.

Connected:

We were not meant to do life alone. Nor are we meant to embark on our own dreams, passions and ventures without a community supporting us. I have had the privilege of meeting some amazing

women through CWI, starting with my first rehearsal for my 2016 SUE Talk.

These women championed who I was, and allowed me to be real and authentic. I have made strong bonds with fellow SUE Talkers, and I feel like I have known some of these women for more than a decade.

Why does it feel so special and comfortable? I can be myself, talk from the heart and discuss real issues that impact my business and my life. That is a connected, well-formed, intentional group. In the wide world of networking, this is a

rare gem. How privileged I am to have become a part of this special group.

Women:

You may think this is fairly self-explanatory. However, let's dive a little deeper. Look at where many of us have come from: corporate America.

We have had to navigate the layers of hierarchy, deal with horrible bosses, and strive to do our best in the midst of office politics, low morale,and distrustful relationships. Many of us have been through layoffs, and this came in the midst of supporting our families and striving to get to the "next level."

We have also had numerous discussions with dream killers: those who mocked our ideas or told us, "Yah, I don't think so" or "Prove yourself first, then come back to me when you have a real business model or revenue." Seriously – how do we get up in the morning and make it through the day without completely losing it?

However—here we are, in a group of other women who have been through similar, daunting circumstances; who survived the fire and came out of it stronger. We can learn from other women who have paved the way for us and are on the journey beside us. In numbers, we have great strength, resilience and hope.

Influence:

We can only be influential if we allow time for authentic relationships to truly take us to the next level. Through CWI, I have met some women who took immediate action via email and introduced me to other tremendous, powerful women. To be influential is to be respected, not necessarily well-liked. We can make a positive impact and contribution to other women – those in high school, and those going through college and getting their first job. Imagine how we can share our stories and perhaps become mentors to help shape these rising women's futures.

So – let's step out, continue to make bold moves and pursue our dreams – together. Let us, as strong women, be connected and influential. Here's to the future of women!

Sashi Whitman is a contributing writer for Women Lead Publications, where she covers all aspects related to empowering young women in their confidence and communication. Sashi is the Co-Founder and CEO of SUE Rising(tm), a non-profit organization centered on creating a lasting legacy of future female leaders. Sashi is also an educator and teaches market research at UCSD Extension for international students, and business and marketing courses at San Diego Miramar College. www.suerising.org

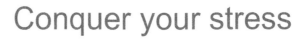

Conquer your stress

We all know that part of being healthy is eating the right foods and moving our bodies every day. Here is a lesser-known way to improve our health right away.

We've all heard that managing our stress is important for our mental health, but science has proven that just managing our stress or removing a stressor isn't enough. The concept of completing the stress cycle goes back to our primitive days and is more powerful than just managing stress or removing the stressor.

The fact is: we encountered the stressor, and our bodies have a physiologic need to convert from our fight or flight response (the stress) to the rest, digest, and restore response. By removing the stressor or deep breathing through a stressful time, we are missing the crucial step of moving from the sympathetic nervous system to the parasympathetic keeping the stress trapped in the tissues, quite literally.

The best way to complete the stress cycle is to move your body.

Imagine thousands of years ago, foraging for food and you stumble upon a bear (stressor). What would you think to do? Run away! The flight part of your fight or flight response would kick in to save your tushy, and when you escaped unscathed, you would have burned off the excess stress hormones that gave you the power to run faster than a bear. You don't have to run to complete the stress cycle, you can move your body in whatever way makes you feel good. Walk, cycle, swim, hike, yoga, Pilates, boxing…the options are endless. Also, studies have shown that a 6-second kiss, or a 20-second hug will also complete the stress cycle. Primitively, once we ran away from the bear, we'd end up with our tribe who'd hug us and comfort us for completing such an amazing feat. Get to moving, hugging, and kissing more; then go conquer the world, my loves!

Sharleen Lawrence is a contributing writer for Women Lead Publications. She is the owner and Chief Executive HypnoPuncturist at Empire Wellness Center. Since 2015, Sharleen has been helping people improve their physical and mental health using cutting edge technology and ancient tools to harmonize their mind, body, and soul. She developed the HypnoPuncture Method by combining hypnosis with acupuncture and has helped transform the lives of hundreds of women by reprogramming their subconscious mind for healing and success. www.empirewellnesscenter.com

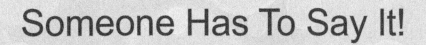

Someone Has To Say It!

"Be a voice not an echo."

"I will not stay silent so that you can stay comfortable."

*"Never be afraid to speak your mind,
you have one for a reason."*
~ Sarah Moores

Don't hit the trees on your way to success

A few years back, I went to Big Bear Mountain with family during the off season. We took our bikes to enjoy some mountain biking. I had at the time, don't laugh, a Huffy bike from the 1980's. I decided, in my adventurous spirit, "Oh hell, I can bike down Big Bear Mountain!".

I get not even 50 feet and I start sliding on the gravel on a 45-degree downgrade. Panic set in.

What am I going to do? I was so scared. But I could not just stay here; I have to get down. So, I changed the channel in my head.

"I can do this! Own this bike! See it happen", me conquering this mountain. I didn't waste time. I envisioned myself riding down, I could see it. In a split second, I took off.

I focused on the path ahead, not the gravel, not the daunting drop or majestic view, just the path. Keep moving. Do not look at the trees. And I made it.

Many times, I get asked, in my professional career, how did I accomplish what I had. And it always bewildered me how to answer. Of course, it's about having knowledge, being professional, working hard, being organized, being passionate, being tenacious, networking, & never giving up on your dreams. But everyone does that. There was something else I did, but I couldn't put my finger on it.

Until it dawned on me. Just like riding down Big Bear Mountain, I focus on the path not the obstacles. **That is how I was successful. My dreams, my passions, light up like a path. I can see it clear as day.** I still see the obstacles, but they are in my peripheral vision, and I conquer each one, one by one.

If I had looked at every obstacle, it would have seemed impossible. Daunting. But when I finally get to the goal, I look back at all the trees I maneuvered around and smile.

Monique Guzman is a contributing writer for Women Lead Publications, where she covers her keys to success. Monique Guzman is a designer & artist. For 11 years, her latest brand, where she handmade, a zero-waste line, one of kind, and mixed art with fashion. Her aim was to make her clients feel beautiful in their skin & save the planet. She took her label down the runways of Portland, New York & London. www.SirenSkirts.com

Word & Brown General Agency is a **proud sponsor** and **supporter** of **Connected Women of Influence.**

Headquartered in Orange, California, Word & Brown has a 35-year history of helping brokers address the diverse health insurance and employee benefits needs of small and large businesses.

Word & Brown delivers innovative sales tools, industry-leading quoting, personalized sales support, a commitment to helping brokers increase sales, and a pledge to *"Service of Unequalled Excellence."*

wordandbrown.com

Good advice
Isn't always good

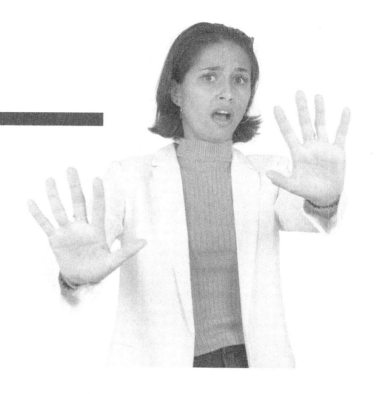

Starting a business is daunting; not easy, fun, or fast. Starting one in the middle of an economic crash in a third world country was even more daunting.

The crash hadn't happened - yet, but the decision to move forward in a third world country was made. I had decided to limit my launch progress to those very close to me. Even they had many doubts for me, some trying to convince me to wait.

At 62, what was I to wait for? I'd never planned on opening a business - ever, but now that the decision was made, I saw no point, no valid reason, in waiting nor taking the advice of well-meaning friends and relatives. Positive comments with a negative spin, are you sure you want to? you know they're known for scamming people, hmmm not sure, it's going to be too expensive to sell to the average person.....these comments began to weigh on me.

I needed to move on and create a new life for myself, after the deaths of my younger brothers.

I could not allow the chatter to sway me.

After all, starting a business was all new to me and I had my own reservations to get past. However, the 'fierce urgency of now' took over....I knew I had to do this. I needed something to soothe my soul, to take away the pain. I needed positive guidance, and well-meaning or not, I couldn't allow the 'good advice' to sway me to move in another direction. Good advice isn't always good and can often be a distraction, which I didn't need.

That huge leap of faith led me to open my business in Tanzania, Africa. I didn't know it would become my passion. I do know that making my own decisions was key to my business becoming the success it is today. Yes, there were times I wondered if I made the right decision, which often gave me pause, but wasn't sufficient enough, because I DID it.

"Safari" Kay Trotman is a contributing writer for Women Lead Publications. Over the years, hundreds of travelers have enjoyed the benefits of an African Safari, led by 'Safari' Kay, President of Destined To Travel. Kay has been spreading the word for the past fourteen years, and educating potential travelers of the decline and disappearance of wildlife in Africa and why, most importantly, she advises taking an African Safari off of your bucket list and putting it on the top of your LIVE list. Keep wildlife wild! www.destined-to-travel.com

What can a female leader bring to a male institution?

I survived thirty years as a female prison doctor in a male prison, controlled by a male militaristic hierarchy. I watched how the leadership impacted male prisoners and staff. In my career I had nine different prison directors and only one of them was a female, Jackie Crawford. She was the first female prison director in Nevada, and her leadership stood out.

She brought with her curiosity, compassion and a flexible mindset, which was opposite the mindset and actions I saw in the male prison directors before and after her. She was not naive or inexperienced, as she had served as a warden in two different states. She knew security and reduction of violence in a prison was paramount, but she approached it differently. **Her solution was not to increase punishment and restrictions which the male directors did, she instead put in place programs to encourage the traits she wanted to see.**

Those programs included the Puppies on Parole Program, the Mustang Program and the Structured Senior Living Program known as True Grit. The inmates could also earn meritorious credits for good behavior in those programs and others, which would reduce the time they would serve.

Taking care of dogs that the SPCA considered unadoptable, gentling mustangs and auctioning them off, and helping the elderly in the True Grit program changed the way the inmates looked at themselves and others. I could see the positive impact on their mental and physical health, and the decrease in violence, because I took care of them. I could also see that they would be less of a risk to society than when they entered, and isn't that what society wants? Jackie was a true leader, because she could see beyond the prison walls and had the courage to lead the way.

Karen Gedney, MD, is a contributing writer for Women Lead Publications. Karen is the author of '30 Years Behind Bars,' Trials of a Prison Doctor. Karen is a speaker, mentor and prison reform activist. www.discoverdrg.com

NATIONAL
women
of *influence*
A W A R D S

connected women
OF INFLUENCE®

Join Us!

Thursday | November 4 | 2021

For details and to nominate or register:
www.womenofinfluenceawards.com

award categories

- **Gamechanger Award**
- **Woman to Watch Award**
- **Women Breaking Barriers Award**
- **Women's Advocate of the Year Award**
- **President's Award**
- **Emerging Woman Owned Business Award**
- **Author of Influence Award**
- **Champion of Women Award**
- **Catalyst Award**
- **Veteran of Influence Award**
- **Lifetime Legacy Award**
- **NextGen Award**
- **Resilience Award**
- **Connected Women of Influence Award**

Bad hair cut

Women are the next wave of wealth transfer – by 2030 we will control an estimated $30 Trillion in assets. According to a Merrill Lynch study, 3 out of 5 women are not confident when it comes to investing and working with the right advisor can educate and empower you to build that confidence.

Why is it important to be educated and empowered? Women tend to outlive men by an average of five years which lead to the need to save more for retirement, so we do not run out of money. This tends to be a challenge even in 2021 as women still only earn on average $0.82 for every $1 a man makes. Not only do we need to save more for a longer period, but we also need to use a greater percentage of our pay to do so. A Fidelity study states when women are educated and invest, they earn on average 40 basis points more than men and add a greater amount to their account balance.

Seventy percent of people will have a long-term event in their life; and if not properly planned for, it can wipe out of lifetime's worth of savings in a flash.

These reasons are why a financial advisor is more important to the health of your financial plan. The right advisor will work with you holistically at all aspects of your financial health, cash flow, debt management, asset protection, asset accumulation and finally estate planning. She'll educate you on the different areas to make sure you understand the recommendations and find a solution that will not only help you achieve your financial goals but will feel comfortable when it comes to

risk. Proper planning also help you leverage your money to save taxes, not pay more.

Lastly, an advisor will help you in times of market volatility and help you take emotion out of the equation and help you stay the course. Think of it this way, would you leave cutting your hair yourself or to a professional?

Not working with an advisor is equivalent to a bad haircut, except to recover is years, not weeks.

Michele Farrell is a contributing writer for Women Lead Publications, where she covers all things to educate and empower women in the financial arena. Her family was struck by the lack of financial education out there and Michele took matters into her own hands by becoming an advisor seven years ago and won the Los Angeles Tribune's Financial of the Year in 2020.

alumni

Deeran Anderson
Anderson & Hooper Business Advisory

Sahar Andrade
Sahar Consulting, LLC

Michelle Beauchamp
The Champ Group

Sylvia Becker-Hill
Becker-Hill Inc.

Michelle Bergquist
Connected Women of Influence

Sherrie Berry
Visage Pro USA

Samantha Bianes
SUE Riser

Chariya Bissonette

Stefanie Blue
TRUE BLUE Branding SD

Billiekai Boughton
San Diego Women Veterans Network

Toni Brooks
Toni Brooks Foundation

John Burroughs
Finance of America

Barbara Burton
The Burton Company

AnGele M. Cade
Executive on the Go, Inc.

Dianne Callahan
Catalyst Coaching & Consulting

Liz Camaur
Camaur Crampton Family Law PC

Knight Campbell
Cairn Leadership Strategies

Lori Chavez-Wysocki
Jack in the Box

Jen Conkey
Warriors of Wealth

Joanie Connell
Flexible Work Solutions

Angelica Cortez
SUE Riser

Christine Cunliffe
Bobo Strategy

Joylyn Darnell
National University

Kathy David
IT TechPros Inc

Erika De La Cruz
Passionistas

Karen Dietz
Just Story it

Mimi Donaldson
MimiSpeaks!

Klyn Elsbury
MK Foundation

Juleen Erives
SUE Riser

Michele Farrell
The Financial Architects

Eldonna Fernandez
Dynamic Vision Int'l Inc.

Windus Fernandez Brinkkord
Trilogy Financial Services

Hillary Gadsby
Stiletto Gal

Mike Giorgione
LeadingLeaders

Cheryl Goodman
SONY North America

Adrienne Grace
Vim & Vigor Creative

Shadoe Gray
Miss Management

Pattie Grimm
Johnson & Johnson Vision

Cheryl Guidry
Safe Dating Over 50

Eve Gumpel
Good Writing Matters

Monique Guzman
Siren Skirts

Lenka Holman
Transamerica Financial Advisors, Inc.

Candise Holmlund

Wendy Hooper Ross
Veracity Real Estate Co.

Lauryn Hunter
Hunter Therapeutic

Scharrell Jackson
Squar Milner LLP

Naomi Jefferson-Glipa
SUE Riser

Rebecca Johannsen
Rebecca Johannsen Consulting

Maria Keckler
Superb Communication

Lucy Kelleher
Keep Them Loyal

Bethany Kelly
Publishing Partner

Colm Kelly
Do Business Smarter

JC Keville
Renewal by Andersen

Jenelle Kim
JBK Wellness Labs

Chris King
Chris M. King

Melanie Klinghoffer
Powerful Transformations

Rhana Kozak
Brighterstep Inc

Erin Krehbiel
Gallagher

Marty Kurner
Hawden Group USA

Lynn Lambrecht
The Living Planner

Gillian Larson
Reality Rally Inc.

Rachel Lee
rachelslee.com

Charlesetta Medina
Titan Women Collective

Analia Mendez
Signature Careers

Liane Monaco Christensen
LP3-SecurIT

Terry Monkaba
Williams Syndrome Assoc.

Robbie Motter
NAFE National Assoc. of Female Entre-preneurs

Sheri Nasim
Center for Executive Excellence, Inc.

Ana Nieto
Mindful Online Workouts

Daniel Olexa
Author, Speaker, Life Coach Trainer

Linda Patten
Dare2Lead with Linda

Philip Pfeifer
Traction Coach

Deanna Potter
Centre For Organization Effectiveness

Jenni Prisk
Prisk Communication

Gina Ray
Good Writing Matters

Jessica Reveles
ABBYY

Andria Schultz
VLin Inc.

Zhe Scott
TSQ Marketing

Jennifer Shen
Chula Vista PD

LaVonne Shields
Management Consultants of America

Tioffani Sierra
Management Consultants of America

Tammy Singer
Improv It Up

Jennifer Stahl-Williams
Jennifer Stahl Events

Lyena Strelkoff
Shero's Journey

Elaine Swann
Elaine Swann Enterprises

Debbra Sweet
Author | Speaker

Elisa Swenson
International Professional Rodeo Assoc.

Deborah Thorne
The Information Diva

MellissaTong
DuckPunk Productions Inc.

Tanya Torres
Merrill Lynch

Susan Treadgold
Treadgold Executive Development

Kay Trotman
Destined to Travel

Quyen Tu
Law Office of Quyen Tu

Julia Uhll
Realty ONE Group

Mary Van Dorn
Van Dorn Mortgage Group

Renee VanHeel
Pay It Forward Processing

Pattie Vargas
The Vargas Group

Eva Vennari
The Elevate Institute

Tracy Ward
Forward Talent

Sashi Whitman
UCSD Extension

Lizzie Wittig
Susan G. Komen, San Diego

Tamsin Woolley-Barker
TEEM Innovation Group; Dr. Tamsin

Debbie Wright
MOTEC Auto Care

Candice Yorke
Behr Paint Co.

Elijah Young
Pains Promise

Catherine Zundel
Civility Partners, LLC

How to be the most powerful leader you can be

All our lives (and for centuries) women have received the message that the qualities which make us feminine are not valued in leadership. "Feminine" qualities are creativity, influence, collaboration, cooperation, compassion, empathy, intuition, patience, vision, passion and "heart."

We learned from an early age to hide many of these qualities. We learned to take on the qualities of the masculine leadership model accepted by society. The "masculine" qualities are "mind" over "heart," command, assertiveness, action, direction and ambition, strength, competitiveness, independence, aggression, and process over vision.

We'd try our best to fit into that mold but we still didn't fit the picture men (and many women) had of what leadership looks like. And, we were suppressing the whole of who we are as people, and the full range of gifts we have to share with the world.

All of these qualities are valuable and appropriate for different situations, and ALL people possess both masculine and feminine qualities to varying degrees.

What would the world be like if everyone could show their qualities and strengths freely and unapologetically?

From decades of studying and training leaders, I believe that the most effective leadership model is a marriage of masculine strengths ("command") and feminine strengths ("influence"). I coined the term Comfluential Leadership™ — command + influence — which allows ALL genders to bring their best strengths out to the world.

Comfluential Leadership™ empowers us to break through gender heritage, redefine what leadership is for us, and to lead more effectively. I teach Comfluential Leadership™ because I strongly believe this is a model we women must master in order to effect the change this world is calling for.

Tapping into her full range of abilities, a woman can truly change the world!

How to take the first step? Embrace your feminine qualities of leadership by recognizing that the masculine model doesn't define you. It will take courage to step into your own model of leadership. But when you do, you will be fully expressing who you are and what you're meant to bring to the world.

It's so worth it, don't you think?

Linda Patten is a contributing writer for Women Lead Publications, where she examines the art of leadership. Linda Patten (MBA) is the founder of Dare2Lead with Linda, an international speaker and best-selling author, radio show host (now syndicated), leadership expert, mentor and trainer to professional associations, major organizations, business networking groups and the military. She is a gifted communicator, who spoke on SUE Talks: Connected Women of Influence. www.dare2leadwithlinda.com

92% of the top earners in the U.S. are men.
95% of Fortune 1000 firms are led by men.
83% of boardroom seats are filled by men.
85% of executive officers are men.

WHAT SHOULD WOMEN DO?

Since men currently hold the power positions in business and industry, has anyone ever asked men what they think women should do to advance in business?

Michelle Bergquist, CEO of Connected Women of Influence, did.

Her book, *How Women Sabotage Their Success in Business,* provides honest, practical, credible advice on how more women can advance in business... according to men!

In this book you will learn how to:

- Play the game of business
- Show results
- Get your brag on
- Know and describe your worth
- Be visible so you get promoted
- Speak up and be noticed
- Turn your ask on
- Be you and learn to adapt
- Search for mentors and advocates
- Support other women for advancement

women lead
PUBLISHING™

brought to you by:

connected women
OF INFLUENCE®

Get your copy today online at Amazon.com

FINANCE *of* AMERICA
— MORTGAGE™—

Mortgage rates are at historic lows!

Take advantage of your potential buying power.

Thinking about buying or refinancing a home?

With rates at historic lows, now might be the time to find out if you qualify for a mortgage from Finance of America Mortgage.

You may want to take advantage of these low rates if you:

- Have been waiting to purchase your first home.
- Want to qualify for a larger loan amount.
- Have been thinking about refinancing your current mortgage.

John Burroughs
Senior Loan Officer
NMLS-238441
o: (760) 944-6555
john.burroughs@financeofamerica.com
FAMadvisor.com/johnburroughs

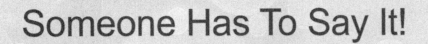

Someone Has To Say It!

"Don't fear confrontation. Fear what happens when you don't speak up for yourself."

"The greatest talent one can have is learning when to speak and when to not."
~ Bryant A. Loney

5 ways to jump into
JOY!

People tend to live their lives in the past or future while running on auto pilot in today. How much time do you spend thinking about the past woulda, coulda and shoulda's and "what if-ing" about the future, can have a significant impact on the quality of your life and your experience of living in the here and now.

Both ways of interacting with your world can cause you to miss out on joy in day-to-day life.

When you focus on living in the present, you give yourself, and others around you, the gift of fully experiencing happiness, joy and life, in each moment today.

5 Tips to Being Present

1) Notice if your thoughts are primarily focused on the past, or future. Where is your attention? Have you ever zoned out while driving on the freeway and notice that you are several exits up the road when you "come to?" You were not in the present moment. Noticing what you are thinking is half the battle.

2) Find effective ways to ground yourself throughout the day. Put down electronics at lunchtime and notice your food. Practice a five minute mindful exercise or just notice where your feet are!

3) Practice listening to what others are saying rather than preparing your response while they are still talking. Make a game out of repeating back what you just heard.

4) Keep a gratitude journal at night of things you are grateful for that happened during the day. When you start to do this, you will notice that your brain starts to look for the positives rather than the negatives of life. I talk about this in my book, "Down the Rabbit Hole & Back".

5) Practice consciously making choices each day that align with your commitments, goals or dreams.

Living here will provide you with a richness in your life that is not able to manifest if you keep your focus on the past or the future. Living in today is a gift, that's why it is called the present. (Eleanor Roosevelt).

Jump into JOY today!

Elisabeth Caetano, M.A., is a contributing writer for Women Lead Publications. Elisabeth is a published author, speaker, professor and business owner of Navigate Changes as a licensed psychotherapist for more than 23 years. She has made appearances on KPBS radio, KUSI television, given numerous talks around San Diego at professional organizations & local businesses. She also volunteers for several local charities. Winner of Author of Influence 2020 award, her book on navigating life changes is available at DowntheRabbitHoleandBack.com or on any e-reader platform. www.DowntheRabbitHoleandBack.com

Your Brand.
It's a personal thing.
It's a personality thing, really.
It's how you connect with prospects and clients,
and how they feel about you and your business.

TrueBlueBrandingSD
is about that personal touch.
Tailoring photoshoots that are polished & professional, providing
Personal Branding & Visual Content
designed for entrepreneurs and business owners like you.
So you can
SHINE ONLINE!

TRUEBLUE
BRANDINGSD.COM

Lifestyle Portraiture   Product Photography   Visual Brand Design   Social Media Strategy

Just "winging it" is not good enough

A company I worked with several years ago spent a lot of money pulling their small sales force (about 20-30 people) out of the field for a meeting at headquarters. The purpose of the meeting was to introduce the company's new products in advance of a users' conference. Busy as they were preparing for the customer event, the executives, including the VP of Sales and the VP of Marketing, hadn't spent much time preparing to present to the sales force.

And, boy, did it show!

The presentations were unorganized, the PowerPoint slides were sloppy, and the executives often contradicted each other.

The VP of Sales actually said, "If you don't like the names of the new products, well, blame [VP of Marketing]; he came up with them."

I was in the room when that happened. I watched the faces of the sales force. They were looking at each other as if to say, "What the hell kind of company do we work for??"

Instead of the strong and cohesive management team they thought they worked for, the sales force got a very different impression of their corporate overlords. Not only did that impression NOT fill them with confidence about the company's longevity in the marketplace, it made them question their loyalty to their employer.

Three very simple rules of thumb can help your company avoid a similar scenario:

1. Carefully consider the messages you want deliver and the impression you want to leave, especially when you're talking to your sales team and/or channel partners. If they're not inspired, your sales will likely suffer.

2. Develop your presentation long before you plan to give it and rehearse it several times. Never, ever, EVER just wing it. The more organized and professional you look, the more inspired your team will be.

3. When it comes to multi-speaker events, coordinate the presentations to create a logical flow of information from one speaker to the next and to avoid any hint of contradiction among speakers. If you don't have the time to coordinate your presentations, get help from someone who can.

Amy Brandais, M.A., is a contributing writer for Women Lead Publications, where she highlights the importance of strategic communications. Amy has been a communications consultant for over 20 years under the moniker "Amy the Writer," helping companies develop strategic solutions to their communication challenges and strengthen their relationships with both internal and external audiences. www.amythewriter.com

Sashi Whitman is CEO and Co-Founder of SUE Rising, a non-profit organization centered on creating a lasting legacy of future female leaders. Sashi is also a Partner with SUE Talks, which brings bold, passionate, and inspiring talks to leaders and members of the business community. She is one of the lead coaches for SUE Talks, working with businesswomen on crafting and preparing their influential talks.

Sashi holds an MBA from San Diego State and a Bachelor's in Psychology and Sociology from UC San Diego. She teaches market research at UCSD Extension for international students, and business and marketing courses at San Diego Miramar College.

Sashi is passionate about empowering young girls and women to build confidence, find their voice and create influence that breaks barriers globally.

The idea for SUE Rising was the result of a very fortuitous lunch meeting between Sashi Whitman, CEO of SUE Rising, and Michelle Bergquist, CEO and Co-Founder of Connected Women of Influence (CWI). As Sashi and Michelle were talking about the future of SUE Talks, the idea came up: why not bring SUE to school?

Quite literally, bring the concept of bold, passionate, and inspiring talks to middle and high school girls! Why wait until you are a successful businesswoman to share your unique journey, passions, and experience?

Over the course of the last two years, the idea for SUE Rising came to fruition—a non-profit organization that would empower young girls and women to build confidence, find their voice and create influence that break barriers globally.

> **The vision of SUE Rising is to create a lasting legacy of future female leaders.**

Quite often during the middle school to high school years in traditional public schools, students do not receive the regular opportunity to improve their verbal communication skills and build their confidence. There is a huge emphasis on STEM, which is important for future career opportunities. However, one of the missing pieces in the education system is being able to verbally communicate a story and experience to an audience.

Between the ages of 8 and 14, a girl's confidence drops by 30%. Three out of four teenage girls worry about falling. One specific way to build up her confidence: Help her get outside of her comfort zone and take risks.

The flagship event that will help get girls out of that comfort zone is SUE Talks Rising, a speaking competition for middle and high school girls. Participants will receive personalized coaching, and will prepare a 6-minute, rehearsed and memorized talk to share with their peers, parents, faculty and staff. Each of these talkers will be competing for an academic scholarship. Each talker will benefit from confidence in writing, the learned skill of public speaking, and delivering an influential talk.

Our Vision:
To create a lasting legacy of future female leaders

Our goal is to build a young woman's **confidence** and **communication** through a **community** of **connections**.

For more information on SUE Rising, visit suerising.org, or contact Sashi Whitman at sashi@suerising.org

To make a donation, visit: https://secure.givelively.org/donate/sue-rising/fund-her-future

Someone Has To Say It!

*"It takes courage to stand up for yourself.
I stand in honor and no longer in fear of speaking out."
Catherine Jane Fisher*

*"Just remember to always be yourself and don't be
afraid to speak your mind or to dream out loud."
- J.A. Redmerski*

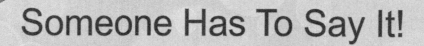

Marketing & strategy that speaks to your customer.

neither over

nor under

Carrie Phair | StatedMarketing.com

women lead
RADIO™

LISTEN LIVE!

MONDAYS | 9 AM | PT

FRIDAYS | 2 PM | PT

iHeart RADIO

Spotify®

Listen on Apple Podcasts

Listen on Google Podcasts

ON AIR

Women Lead Radio produces weekly radio shows dedicated to showcasing successful women CEOs, executives, authors, owners, professionals and companies who support professional women on a variety of business-related topics.

Our dynamic show hosts bring you interviews with thought leaders and insights on topics ranging from money matters to leadership; SEO and online marketing to recruiting; business to health; influence to adventure; reputation to living the lighthearted life.

Join us!

Women Lead Radio Hosts

Kimberley Ausgood

Smart Money Moves

Michelle Bergquist

Women Leading The Way

John Burroughs

Financial Fitness

Dianne Callahan

The Lighthearted Life

Knight Campbell

The Leading Edge

Barbara Eldridge

Trend Setting Women

Michele Farrell

Michele Knows Money

Eileen Gaffen

Reputation And Influence

Shelly Harrison

Amplify Your Influence

Zhe Scott

Getting Down To Business With SEO

Chris King

The Status Flow

Janet Kunst

Ingredients To Online Marketing Success

Rebecca Massoud

Savvy, Soulful And Successful

Leesa McNealy

SpotLite On Recruiting

Donna Netwig

Women On The Journey

Eva Vennari

Owning Your Health

Past shows available online
www.WomenLeadRadio.com

The best souvenirs – even from a journey through illness

I have a photo on my bookcase that reminds me of the most unforgettable trip I've ever taken. It's of me and my best friend, Nan, floating down the Martha Brae River in Jamaica while we were on a wild rum-soaked vacation celebrating my graduation from college in 1988. It's the perfect souvenir of that trip – the first of many journeys taken with my BFF during a friendship now in its 43rd year and going strong.

For the last 14 years Nan has been with me on a different kind of journey - one we never planned or wished for with an often uncertain destination. This has been a journey through illness which began in 2007 when I was diagnosed with aggressive Stage IV non-Hodgkin lymphoma.

On this journey, instead of fruity cocktails with little umbrellas in them, you get chemo cocktails with warnings on them (and coincidentally too much of either cocktail will have you heaving up your guts). Instead of taking in beautiful sunny vistas you spend your time looking at dreary hospital walls. Instead of packing cute outfits for fun activities you get to wear "designer" hospital gowns and scarves to cover up your bald head. But both kinds of journeys do have one thing in common – you have the opportunity to bring back some pretty awesome souvenirs if you look in the right places.

Here are some of the souvenirs I have taken from my journey.

Scars

For some, scars may be unwanted souvenirs reminding them of the pain they've gone through. I have many scars from surgeries and treatments and often felt this way, too, until a friend shared with me the centuries-old Japanese tradition of Kintsugi - the art of fixing broken objects with gold. In this tradition, the flaw is seen as a unique part of the object's history and the repair revitalizes it with new life, making it even more beautiful and valuable. After three tough battles with cancer I, too, have been revitalized with new life and I choose to look at these scars as beautiful souvenirs that remind me of how valuable life is.

Strength

Have you seen the popular Facebook meme "You never know how strong you are until being strong is your only choice"? This is never more true than when you are on your own journey through illness (as the patient or co-traveler). When you are just starting out on the journey you wonder whether you will have the strength to get through it. And day by day, test by test, you do get through it until one day you realize you are stronger than you ever knew and you can face almost anything. It makes me think of the scene in Forrest Gump where Lt. Dan is on the shrimp boat tied to the rigging in the middle of a hurricane yelling out to God "Is that all you got?".

You've made peace with the journey. You've proven to yourself you can handle what life throws at you. You have the strength. That's a priceless souvenir.

Purpose

I believe that the painful and hard times we go through are really on-the-job training for God's greater purposes. For me, turning my own journey through illness into a way to help others gives meaning to this experience. We all know about PTSD – post traumatic stress disorder – but did you know there is an opposite phenomenon called post traumatic growth? This is what happens when you take the souvenir of purpose and use it to make a difference in your own life and the lives of others. It's what Candy Lightner did when she founded MADD, Mothers Against Drunk Driving, after her 13-year old daughter was killed by a drunk driver.

We may not be able to start an international movement like MADD (attributed with saving 350,000+ lives since 1980), but each of us can turn our own journeys into powerful souvenirs that bring light and help and hope to our own corner of the world.

Dianne Callahan is a contributing writer for Women Lead Publications. She is a writer, speaker, philanthropist, and Principal of Catalyst Coaching and Consulting, a high performance coaching company. DIanne is Partner in Women Lead Publishing and her radio show "The Lighthearted Life" is produced by Women Lead Radio. She is a 3-time cancer survivor and was recently named National All-Star Woman of the Year by the Leukemia & Lymphoma Society for her fundraising efforts. Her first book, "Lighthearted Life: Simple strategies to live a joy-filled life even in the stormiest times", is available on Amazon. Her second book, "Journey Through Illness", will be published this year. www.highperformancepowerhour.com

Sale away.
Connect every day.

Take a look at the calendar. When do you see "SALE" signs plastered on shop windows? Chances are if you're in the United States they come in a torrent during the straggly months of the year starting in the fall with Back to School specials, bulk buys of Halloween candy and inflatable lawn ghosts, fancy Thanksgiving meals, and the fateful Black Friday through the whole cyber week of #saledays and #givingdays. As business owners, we do a great job of promoting the back half of the year, but we neglect the days in between. This in turn means we focus on discounting and promotions versus actively building customer loyalty each day.

The goal of marketing is to create awareness and connection between a product and service and a person. It's about relationships, longevity, and trust. It should not be about the transaction. Hence why it feels so important for businesses to work on a year-round calendar of connections that pique interest, build desire, educate and ultimately satisfy a customer's desires. As the owner of a small marketing business, Stated, this is a totally self-serving notion that one should wisely advertise all year round, but also factual! This late boom and dependence on a tight buying cycle create incredible pressure not only on marketing budgets but on operations. It also hurts customers when we mask our sales demands with suspiciously-timed goodwill messages around the holidays.

If we really want to build community and we are invested in long-term relationships then we should support, service, and build our following each day.

A consistent sustained message may not be glamorous but it lengthens the window of opportunity to expose, educate, and endear your audience. With the same dedication, we then look to develop tentpole occasions that resonate with the brand and audience and drive further connection, and are ownable. Like Amazon Prime Day or a floral company creating unique arrangements in January to let moms know their importance year-round. These give us capstone moments that bring in new followers, reward the existing ones, and bring delight during unexpected windows.

I'm not saying we shouldn't take advantage of holiday sales, but what I'd love to see is more businesses being open for creative business every day and rethinking the calendar around what's important to those we serve.

Carrie Phair is a contributing writer for Women Lead Publications. She is the sole proprietor of Stated, a marketing consulting firm partnering with small and medium-sized brands as the CMO to create smarter, insightful, and compelling outreach at every stage of the funnel and on any budget. Inspired by two entrepreneurial parents, backed by a degree in economics, an MBA, and Fortune 20 experience and governed by efficiency and efficacy, Carrie brings pep, strategy, and clarity to the myriad of marketing options. www.statedmarketing.com

Myths about exercise

IT'S ESSENTIAL TO MOVE THE BODY, YES. IT'S EVEN MORE ESSENTIAL TO CONSIDER A HEALTHY FRAMEWORK.

We've all experienced gym class in school or maybe had the benefit of a personal trainer and heard the cries of coaches, "Push" "Make it count" "One more rep" "No pain, no gain!"

It's meant as motivation to help you reach a goal you might not otherwise reach without encouragement. And that's great for a body that's feeling good, is able to repair from being pushed, and isn't experiencing a myriad of symptoms. If that describes you, you can stop reading.

But if you experience a cycle of wanting to work out, injuring yourself, needing to rest from the injury, and starting the cycle over again, read on. You may be working under one or many of the myths below.

MYTH #1:
Strong muscles and a beautiful body indicate you are in good health

MYTH #2:
A healthy heart and healthy arteries indicate you are healthy

MYTH #3:
Exercise rebuilds your body

MYTH #4:
Exercise cannot be harmful

Here are a few guidelines for exercise:

1. Don't use your pulse as your only guide.

2. Follow common sense. Don't push past exhaustion.

3. Don't use exercise as a crutch or drug.

4. If you skip exercise for a few days, you should still feel very well.

6. Involve your whole body.

Walking, swimming, bicycling and gardening are excellent. Long-lived people in the world often work outside, but usually not strenuously. Meditative exercises such as yoga or tai chi are also okay but be careful because many are injured in these classes due to peer pressure to keep up with their classmate's performance rather than focusing on where they are as an individual. The teacher must walk around the entire class at all times to make sure the students are doing the poses correctly at all times. This is very important to avoid injuries. This is why walking is often better, as it is safer.

Eva Vennari is a contributing writer for Women Lead Publications. Eva is a certified Nutritional Counselor in Mineral Balancing and Hair Mineral Analysis supported by Near Infrared Sauna Therapy. She is also certified in Personal Nutrition, Chakra Healing, Akashic Record Reading, and soon to be certified as a M.I.N.D.S. Holistic Alternative Psychology Master Practitioner. www.theElevateInstitute.com

Lighthearted Life Media

Dianne Callahan
CEO, Lighthearted Life Media
909.648.5171
diannecallahan@yahoo.com

LightheartedLife.org

Proud sponsor of Connected Women of Influence.

NEED HELP WITH YOUR GRAPHIC DESIGN, COPYWRITING & BRANDING?

Dianne Callahan is an award-winning communicator and graphic designer. She can help you make your brand stand out to the audiences you are trying to reach!

Businesses call on Dianne to create:

- Brand style guides
- Workbooks
- Forms
- Awards & Giveaways
- Invitations
- PR pieces
- Posters & Banners
- eBooks
- Catalogs
- Social media posts
- Notecards
- Training events
- Postcards
- Celebrations
- Promotional products
- Trade show materials

Connected Womenof Influence Guiding Principles:

We Believe in the Power Of. . .

Why: Because nobody cares what you do.....but we care a whole bunch in "why" you do what you do.

We vs. Me: Because we're strong alone, but fearless together.

Respect: Because people matter. We are all in the people business.

Initiative: We celebrate professional women who take charge and act on ideas and plans with energy, zest and the desire to progressively move forward in business.

Ambition: We champion ambitious women who want to get ahead in business. . .who know what they want... and then go after it.

Extraordinary Openness: Because being authentic and real builds the bridge to powerful, high-performing relationships that lead to extraordinary opportunity and results.

No Judgment: Yep.......SO powerful, it's worth repeating. We truly believe in NO JUDGMENT. Our focus is to support one another and to be true advocates on behalf of each other.

Serve First: Because when you give a little first. . . you get a whole lot in return.

The 'Big Ask': You gotta ask. Because if you don't ask, you don't get. Period. End of story.

Interested in applying for membership?
https://connectedwomenofinfluence.com/cwi-membership/

Habits that help women investors succeed

Intuition. Patience. Discipline. A desire to learn.

These are traits many women naturally possess that can lead to confident decision-making and courageous accomplishments.

They're also the foundation that can help build a sound investing strategy. Perhaps you bootstrapped your own business, broke through the glass ceiling, managed the home front, or benefited from an inheritance. However you got to this point, your collective experience provides the wisdom to help you boldly move forward. But that doesn't mean doing it alone.

Working with a financial advisor and tax team who complements your investing style and listens more than talks, can help you continue making those confident decisions and keep your investment plan on track.

Holistic wealth planning that helps prepare you for the unexpected. When highly emotional life events happen, like divorce, death of a spouse, or even an inheritance, it can be challenging to factor in the financial implications. If one (or more) of these scenarios becomes your reality, it can be a huge relief to have your team already in place. That team can help you navigate difficult decisions that could have an impact on you and your family for years to come.

Just in case, it's best to be prepared and proactive:

• Be aware of your family's assets, debts, retirement accounts, insurance policies, and other financial information.

• Gather important financial documents and safety deposit box keys and keep them accessible.

• Make sure you and your spouse or partner have up-to-date wills and trusts, and that you discuss potential tax implications with your CPA and financial team.

The right fit can make all the difference.

Life hums along and then… something changes. Perhaps you initiated the change or maybe you had to react to it. Either way, having resources to help you navigate decision-making can help mean smoother sailing.

Considering all the aspects of life that have a financial implication is like a wave that keeps expanding.

From investing for a home, college costs, or retirement, to exploring lending and insurance options, an experienced financial team can help you manage risk while keeping you on track toward your investment goals.

Marah Fineberg-Kuck, CFP(r) CRPC(r), *is a contributing writer for Women Lead Publications. This article was written for Wells Fargo Advisors and provided courtesy of Marah Fineberg-Kuck CFP(r) CRPC(r) Marah B. Fineberg-Kuck, CFP(r), is the Executive Director & Founder of the Womens Symposium of Southern California (WSSC), established in 2016. www.wssocal.org*

Color my world perfect

If you miss the mark on something, do you accuse yourself of not being good enough and ruminate on it for days? Do you compare your life to others and think you're not as smart, pretty, fit, or happy enough? Do you feel like you must be 100% perfect 100% of the time?

Perfectionism largely affects women because we are more likely than men to experience feelings of inadequacy at home and work. And, it gets worse. For example, studies suggest that most women only apply for a job when they feel they have 100% of the qualifications, while men apply when having met only 50%.

Perfectionism can cause anxiety, panic attacks, depression, and even eating disorders. Perfectionism starts at an early age and is a huge problem for young girls and women in America. Sadly, over 65% of high school girls are on a diet to lose weight.

Janice, a director of communications, summed it up; "I had to get off social media. It was getting to the point where I thought it was damaging my health. I deleted my Instagram and Facebook accounts because I would get depressed when I saw friends who looked better than me or were doing amazing things in life. The pressure to be perfect was at the heart of my depression. I am educated with a good perspective on life, but it was killing me to see so many of my friends living perfect lives. I was feeling worthless and isolated compared to them."

So how do we combat our need to be perfect? Many psychologists advise that it's important for a woman to know that it's one thing to be her best and another to be perfect. If you suffer from life's perfectionistic curse, do a simple reality check. Take stock of your life and ask yourself if you constantly try to be perfect all the time. If so, study why this may be happening and think about some strategies to overcome your need to be perfect. And finally, make a habit of adopting the words "pretty good" into your mental vocabulary.

Marilou Ryder i*s a contributing writer for Women Lead Publications, where she is a university professor, and best-selling author. She is a passionate proponent of women and girl's empowerment through evidence-based techniques. Through her writing, speaking, and research, she galvanizes others to summon their best selves to approach life's challenges by accessing their personal power. Her innovative work includes the publication of three INSTAGRAPHICS, engaging books infused with Inspirations, Hints, Tips & Truths. SHOW YOUR WORTH, GIRL is her latest Instagraphic for teen girls- available on Amazon. www.drmarilouryder.com*

Brand yourself for success

A groundbreaking Australian study based on years of gender reporting to the federal Workplace Gender Equality Agency, has shown that companies that appointed a female CEO, boosted their market value by 5%. When the number of women in key leadership positions reached or exceeded 10%, the company's market value increased by 6.6%.

This study proves that women are exceptional assets to business, yet many women lack the self-confidence to advance to leadership positions. Internal obstacles often hold them back, they include our desire to be liked; our insecurity about speaking-up during meetings; or our lack of confidence in our skills and expertise.

Thinking like a leader begins by building an internal framework and developing guiding principles that give us the confidence to be decisive, and the clarity to remain focused on our goals.

Develop your success strategy:

• Build a solid foundation by assessing your skills. Make a list of everything you are good at.

• Identify ways to build on your strengths to improve your performance.

• Demonstrate your capabilities -- volunteer to take on responsibilities that utilize your strengths.

• Find a mentor or a coach to help you minimize mistakes and overcome challenges.

• Build a support group of allies who will keep you focused on your goals and encourage you in seeking challenges and overcoming barriers.

Develop your personal brand:

• Respond to voicemail and email messages in a timely manner.

• Complete projects on time. If something comes up that will make it impossible to meet the deadline, inform the other party and agree on a revised due date.

• Follow-up when a project has been completed, send a brief email to confirm that it is done.

• Take on additional responsibilities that will allow you to demonstrate your leadership skills.

• Develop your emotional intelligence and your ability to get along well with others. Excellent interpersonal skills will also increase the likelihood that you will be given a leadership role.

• Publicize your accomplishments to teams, key managers and executive personnel.

Branding yourself as an effective, reliable, productive employee is among the most valuable strategies to advance your career.

Kimberlee Centera is a contributing writer for Women Lead Publications. She is the CEO of TerraPro Solutions, a leading risk management expert for the development and financing of utility scale renewable energy projects. She is a contributor to North American Clean Energy and the Norton Rose Fulbright Currents Podcast. Kimberlee has been a guest on numerous radio programs including National Public Radio's Marketplace. She frequently serves as a speaker and educator at wind and solar conferences. www.terraprosolutions.com

Are you SUE?

SUE is on a journey.

SUE is a phoenix rising from the ashes.

SUE can look back, but doesn't let the past hold her back.

SUE has not yet reached her full potential, but is on the path to do so.

SUE does not run alone—she is in community with others for sanity and success.

SUE is real—she is authentic and vulnerable.

SUE is a dreamer, and a hard worker.

SUE is a humble leader, serves others and is passionate about her goals and ambitions.

SUE is successful, she is unstoppable and she is helping to empower other women and girls.

Are you **SUE**?

- Sashi Whitman

Someone Has To Say It!

"When we speak we are afraid our words will not be heard or welcomed. But when we are silent, we are still afraid. So it is better to speak."

"Don't be afraid to be unique or speak your mind, because that's what makes you different from everyone else."
~ Dave Thomas

thank you!

Chairman Sponsors

 Microsoft

 NATIONAL UNIVERSITY

 University of Phoenix

Design

 WALDEN WEALTH MANAGEMENT

 CHILD ENTERTAINMENT

INVERSE PRO AUDIO

Director Sponsors

 Klarinet

 TRUEBLUE BRANDINGSD.COM

 LUMINARY LEADERS

 Word&Brown.

 LightheartedLife.org

 THE CENTRE FOR ORGANIZATION EFFECTIVENESS

 INSIGHT CREDIT GROUP INC

 MIND MASTERS
THE ENTREPRENEURS BRAINSTORMING TEAM

 Mandy Mixes DJ & MC

 DSA

Stated.

 bobo

AMY THE WRITER

 DISTINCTIVE SERVICES

keep them loyal

FORWARD

 SKY SOLUTIONS

THE SEO QUEEN

MARCY BROWE PHOTOGRAPHY

YOUR CONNECTION CONSULTANT

 CALIFORNIA STATE UNIVERSITY FULLERTON

AM

Premier Level Sponsors

 FINANCE of AMERICA — MORTGAGE —

 ELEVATE INSTITUTE

 WEALTHWAVE

Ian Mausner
Savvi Philanthropic LLC

 HB HUTCHINSON and BLOODGOOD LLP

Community Partners

 PIVOT POINT Advantage

 WSSC

 TEAM Referral Network

 GSFE

Women's Business Enterprise Council WEST

Media Partners

 WomensRadio

 Lioness

Publication Designed By
Dianne Callahan, Lighthearted Life Media
Partner, Women Lead Publishing

SUE Talks | Talks that inspire change.™ | Inland Empire 2021 | "Someone Has To Say It"

Made in the USA
Middletown, DE
12 August 2021

45822220R00044